Quot
P.

Compiled and Introduced by

PROINSIAS Mac AONGHUSA

With a Foreword by

SEÁN Mac BRIDE

THE MERCIER PRESS

DUBLIN and CORK

The Mercier Press Limited
25 Lower Abbey Street, Dublin 1
4 Bridge Street, Cork

Quotations from P. H. Pearse:
Compilation and Introduction,
    © Proinsias Mac Aonghusa, 1979.

Reprinted 1979

ISBN 0 85342 605 8

*The publishers are grateful to the Cashel Pearse Centenary Committee
who suggested the idea for this book.*

Printed in the Republic of Ireland
    by Litho Press Co., Midleton, Co. Cork.

FOREWORD

'I have turned my face
to this road before me
To the deed that I see
and the death I shall die.'

(Renunciation, P. H. Pearse, 1916)

Sir John Maxwell, the General Officer commanding the British forces in Ireland, cabled to Asquith, then Prime Minister, advising him not to agree to return the bodies of Pádraic and Willie Pearse to their family in these words: 'Irish sentimentality will turn these graves into martyrs' shrines to which annual processions will be made which would cause constant irritation in this country'.

The letter from Pádraic Pearse to his mother, and two poems dated 1 May 1916, were suppressed by the British authorities. Sir John Maxwell submitted copies to the British Prime Minister saying that some of the content was 'objectionable'.

It is well that a century after Pádraic Pearse's birth his writings should be republished. As Pearse had foreseen, some who considered themselves 'wise' have proclaimed that Pearse's cause was a failure. Others, whose own standards of nationality and freedom do not measure up to those of Pearse, have sought to denigrate him. Still others have tried to depict him as a narrow-minded insular nationalist. Others again have portrayed him as an impractical idealist. Pearse's writings, poems, short stories, plays and political essays provide the answer to all those who speak in 'dispraise' of him. 'Dispraise' is a word he used himself in his last poem when he warned his mother that many would

3

criticise him.

Apart from these considerations the writings of Pearse are of considerable literary value, a value which, so far, has not been adequately recognised. Perhaps in the present era of decadence, Pearse's writings may help to restore some moral values to our world, and to rekindle an ideal for our nation. A nation without an ideal is like a man without a soul.

Seán MacBride

INTRODUCTION

PATRICK HENRY PEARSE
1879 - 1916

Patrick Henry Pearse, or Pádraic Mac Píarais as he is known
in Irish, has had more influence on the Ireland of the
twentieth century than any other person. The very fact that
sixty years and more after his execution by an English
firing squad clever men should spend time and energy
devising ways in which to denigrate him speaks for itself.
P. H. Pearse, an Englishman's son, spoke for the resurgent
people of Ireland in clearer and more unmistakable words
than even those patriots whom he himself revered. He was a
teacher in the very best sense. He was a poet. He was a
writer of fine prose both in Irish and in English. He was
foremost in efforts to ensure that the Irish language would
neither wither away nor die. He was a splendid orator. He
was a Separatist. He was a patriot. He spoke for generations
past and generations to come when he declared at the grave
of the Fenian O'Donovan Rossa 'Ireland unfree shall never
be at peace'.

One hundred years after his birth in Dublin it is fitting
that a small volume of quotations from the writings of this
extraordinary Irishman should be readily available. Let it be
for readers but an introduction to all of his writings.

Proinsias Mac Aonghusa
26 February, 1979

5

QUOTATIONS FROM P. H. PEARSE

We have come to the holiest place in Ireland; holier to us even than the place where Patrick sleeps in Down. Patrick brought us life, but this man died for us. And though many before him and some since have died in testimony of the truth of Ireland's claim to nationhood, Wolfe Tone was the greatest of all that have made that testimony, the greatest of all that have died for Ireland whether in old times or in new. He was the greatest of Irish Nationalists; I believe he was the greatest of Irish men. And if I am right in this I am right in saying that we stand in the holiest place in Ireland, for it must be that the holiest sod of a nation's soil is the sod where the greatest of her dead lies buried.

Address delivered at the Grave of Wolfe Tone in
Bodenstown Churchyard, Co. Kildare, 22 June 1913

To his teaching we owe it there is such a thing as Irish Nationalism and to the memory of the deed he nerved his generation to do, to the memory of '98, we owe it that there is any manhood left in Ireland.

Ibid.

Think of Tone... Think of how he put virility into the Catholic movement, how this heretic toiled to make free men of Catholic helot, how as he worked among them he grew to know and love the real, the historic Irish people, and the great, clear, sane conception came to him that in

Ireland there must be not two nations or three nations but one nation, that Protestant and Dissenter must be brought into amity with Catholic and that Catholic, Protestant and Dissenter must unite to achieve freedom for all.

Ibid.

And let us make no mistake as to what Tone sought to do, what it remains to us to do. We need to restate our programme: Tone has stated it for us:

> To break the connection with England, the never-failing source of all our political evils, and to assert the independence of my country—these were my objects. To unite the whole people of Ireland, to abolish the memory of all past dissentions, and to substitute the common name of Irishmen in place of the denominations of Protestant, Catholic and Dissenter—these were my means.

I find here implicit all the philosophy of Irish nationalism, all the teaching of the Gaelic League and the later prophets. Ireland one and Ireland free—is not this the definition of Ireland a Nation? To that definition and to that programme we declare our adhesion anew; pledging ourselves as Tone pledged himself—and in this sacred place, by this graveside, let us not pledge ourselves unless we mean to keep our pledge—we pledge ourselves to follow in the steps of Tone, never to rest either by day or night until his work be accomplished, deeming it the proudest of all privileges to fight for freedom, to fight not in despondency but in great joy hoping for the victory in our day, but fighting on whether victory seem near or far, never lowering our ideal, never bartering one jot or tittle of our birthright, holding faith to the memory and the inspiration of Tone, and accounting ourselves base as long as we endure the evil thing against which he testified with his blood.

Ibid.

And our patriotism is measured not by the formula in which we declare it but by the service which we render. We owe to our country all fealty and she asks always for our service; and there are times when she asks of us not ordinary but some supreme service. There are in every generation those who shrink from the ultimate sacrifice, but there are in every generation those who make it with joy and laughter and these are the salt of the generations, the heroes who stand midway between God and man.

Address delivered at the Robert Emmet Commemoration in the Academy of Music, Brooklyn, New York, 2 March 1914.

No failure judged as the world judges such things was ever more complete, more pathetic than Emmet's. And yet he has left us a prouder memory than the memory of Brian victorious at Clontarf or of Owen Roe victorious at Benburb. It is the memory of a sacrifice Christ-like in its perfection. Dowered with all things splendid and sweet he left all things and elected to die. Face to face with England in the dock at Green Street he uttered the most memorable words ever uttered by an Irish man: words which rising clear above a century's tumults forbid us ever to waver or grow weary until our country takes her place among the nations of the earth. And his death was august. In the great space of Thomas Street an immense silent crowd; in front of St Catherine's Church a gallows upon a platform; a young man climbs to it, quiet, serene, almost smiling, they say—ah, he was very brave; there is no cheer from the crowd, no groan; this man is to die for them but no man dares to say aloud 'God bless you, Robert Emmet'. Dublin must one day wash out in blood the shameful memory of that quiescence.

Ibid.

Emmet redeemed Ireland from acquiescence in the Union. His attempt was not a failure but a triumph for that deathless thing we call Irish Nationality. It was by Emmet that men remembered Ireland until Davis and Mitchell took up the work again, and '48 handed on the tradition to '67 and from '67 we receive the tradition unbroken.

Ibid.

I have said again and again that when the Gaelic League was founded in 1893 the Irish Revolution began.

Ibid.

After all there are in Ireland two parties: those who stand for the English connection and those who stand against it.

Ibid.

In every generation we have renewed the struggle and so it shall be unto the end. When England thinks she has trampled out our battle in blood some brave man rises and rallies us again; when England thinks she has purchased us with a bribe some good man redeems us by a sacrifice. Whenever England goes on her mission of empire we meet her and we strike at her; yesterday it was on the South African veldt, today it is in the Senate House at Washington, tomorrow it may be in the streets of Dublin. We pursue her like a sleuth-hound; we lie in wait for her and come upon her like a thief in the night; and some day we will overwhelm her with the wrath of God.

Address delivered at the Robert Emmet Commemoration in the Aeolian Hall, New York, 9 March 1914.

I think I can speak for a younger generation still: for some

10

of the young men that are entering the National University, for my own pupils at St Enda's College, for the boys of Fianna Éireann. To the grey-haired men whom I see on this platform, to John Devoy and Richard Burke, I bring them then this message from Ireland: that their seed-growing of forty years ago has not been without its harvest, that there are young men and little boys in Ireland today who remember what they taught and who with God's blessing will one day take—or make—an opportunity of putting their teaching into practice.

Ibid.

A European war has brought about a crisis which may contain as yet hidden within it the moment for which the generations have been waiting. It remains to be seen whether if that moment reveals itself we shall have the sight to see and the courage to do, or whether it shall be written of this generation alone of all the generations of Ireland, that it had none among it who dared to make the ultimate sacrifice.

Note made in August, 1914

If we do not believe in the divinity of our people we have no business or very little all these years in the Gaelic League. In fact if we had not believed in the divinity of our people we should in all probability not have gone into the Gaelic League at all. We should have made our peace with the Devil, and perhaps might have found him a very decent sort; for he liberally rewards with attorney-generalships, bank balances, villa residences and so forth the great and the little who serve him well.

The Coming Revolution, November, 1913

11

There will be in the Ireland of the next few years a multi-tudinous activity of Freedom Clubs, Young Republican Parties, Labour Organisations, Socialist Groups and what not; bewildering enterprises undertaken by sane persons and insane persons, but good men and bad men, many of them seemingly contradictory, some mutually destructive, yet all tending towards a common objective and that objective: the Irish Revolution.

Ibid.

For if there is one thing that has become plainer than another it is that when the seven men met in O'Connell Street to found the Gaelic League there were commencing, had there been a Liancourt there to make the epigram, not a revolt but a revolution.

Ibid.

Whenever Dr Hyde, at a meeting at which I have had a chance of speaking after him, has produced his dove of peace I have always been careful to produce my sword; and to tantalise him by saying that the Gaelic League has brought into Ireland 'Not Peace, but a Sword'. But this does not show any fundamental difference of outlook between my leader and me; for while he is thinking of peace between brother Irishmen I am thinking of the sword-point between banded Irishmen and the foreign force that occupies Ireland: and his peace is necessary to my war. It is evident that there can be no peace between the body politic and a foreign substance that has intruded itself into its system: between them war only until the foreign substance is expelled or assimilated.

Ibid.

A thing that stands demonstrable is that nationhood is not achieved otherwise than in arms: in one or two instances there may have been no actual bloodshed but the arms were there and the ability to use them. Ireland unarmed will attain just as much freedom as it is convenient for England to give her; Ireland armed will attain ultimately just as much freedom as she wants.

Ibid.

Parnell. . . the one really great Nationalist of his time: the true successor of Tone and Mitchell, though working with such different means.

The Psychology of a Volunteer, January, 1914.

Parnell as a leader of the Irish in their struggle for nationhood would not have been justified in devoting one hour of his time or one penny of his funds to the land war except as a means to an end. Had Parnell had his way the land war would not have been found out until the national war had been won: and it is a pity that Parnell had not his way, as we and our children may realise full soon.

Ibid.

I propose that in future we reserve the term Palesman for those who uphold the domination of the English in Ireland. I propose also that we substitute for the denominations Gael, Gall and Gall-Gael the common name of Irishman.

Ibid.

We believe as every Irish boy whose heart has not been corrupted by foreign influence must believe that our country ought to be free. We do not see why Ireland should allow England to govern her, either through Englishmen as at present or through Irishmen under an appearance of self-government. We believe that England has no business in this country at all—that Ireland from the centre to the zenith belongs to the Irish. Our forefathers believed this and fought for it: Hugh O'Donnell and Hugh O'Neill and Rory O'More and Owen Roe O'Neill: Tone and Emmet and Davis and Mitchel. What was true in their time is still true. Nothing that has happened or that can ever happen can alter the truth of it. Ireland belongs to the Irish. We believe then that it is the duty of Irishmen to struggle always, never giving in or growing weary until they have won back their country again.

To the Boys of Ireland, February, 1914.

O'Donovan Rossa was not the greatest man of the Fenian generation but he was its most typical man. He was the man that to the masses of his countrymen then and since stood most starkly and plainly for the Fenian idea. More lovable and understandable than the cold and enigmatic Stephens, better known than the shy and sensitive Kickham, more human than the scholarly and chivalrous O'Leary, more picturesque than the able and urbane Luby, older and more prominent than the man who when the time comes to write his biography will be recognised as the greatest of the Fenians—John Devoy—Rossa held a unique place in the hearts of Irish men and Irish women. They made songs about him, his very name passed into a proverb. To avow oneself a friend of O'Donovan Rossa meant in the days of our fathers to avow oneself a friend of Ireland, an 'Irish enemy', an 'Irish savage', if you will, naked and unashamed. Rossa was not only 'extreme', but he represented the left wing of the 'extremists'. Not only would he have Ireland free but he would have Ireland Gaelic.

O'Donvan Rossa, A Character Study, July, 1915

And here we have the secret of Rossa's magic, of Rossa's power: he came out of the Gaelic tradition. He was of the Gael; he thought in a Gaelic way; he spoke in Gaelic accents. He was the spiritual and intellectual descendant of Colm Cille and of Seán an Díomais. With Colm Cille he might have said, 'If I die it shall be from the love I bear the Gael'; with Shane O'Neill he held it debasing to 'twist his mouth with English'. To him the Gael and the Gaelic ways were splendid and holy, worthy of all homage and all service; for the English he had a hatred that was tinctured with contempt. He looked upon them as an inferior race, morally and intellectually; he despised their civilisation; he mocked at their institutions and made them look ridiculous.

Ibid.

And this again explains why the English hated him above all the Fenians. They hated him as they hated Shane O'Neill and as they hated Parnell; but more. For the same 'crime' against English law as his associates he was sentenced to a more terrible penalty; and they pursued him into his prison and tried to break his spirit by mean and petty cruelty. He stood up to them and fought them: he made their whole penal system odious and despicable in the eyes of Europe and America. So the English found Rossa in prison a more terrible foe than Rossa at large; and they were glad at last when they had to let him go. Without any literary pretentions his story of his prison life remains one of the sombre epics of the earthly inferno.

Ibid.

I propose to you then that here by the grave of this unrepentant Fenian we renew our baptismal vows; that here by the grave of this unconquered and unconquerable man we ask of God, each one for himself, such unshakable purpose,

such high and gallant courage, such unbreakable strength of
soul as belonged to O'Donovan Rossa.

*Oration at the grave of O'Donovan Rossa
at Glasnevin, Dublin, 1 August, 1915.*

Deliberately here we avow ourselves, as he avowed himself
in the dock, Irishmen of one allegiance only. We of the Irish
Volunteers and you others who are associated with us in
today's task and duty are bound together and must stand
together henceforth in brotherly union for the achievement
of the freedom of Ireland. And we know only one definition of freedom: it is Tone's definition, it is Mitchel's definition, it is Rossa's definition. Let no man blaspheme the
cause that the dead generations of Ireland served by giving
it any other name and definition than their name and their
definition.

Ibid.

Splendid and holy causes are served by men who are themselves splendid and holy. O'Donovan Rossa was splendid in
the proud manhood of him, splendid in the heroic grace of
him, splendid in the Gaelic strength and clarity and truth of
him. And all that splendour and pride and strength was
compatible with a humility and a simplicity of devotion to
Ireland, to all that was olden and beautiful and Gaelic in
Ireland, the holiness and simplicity of patriotism of a
Michael O'Clery or of an Eoghan O'Growney. The clear
true eyes of this man almost alone in his day visioned Ireland as we of today would surely have her: not free merely
but Gaelic as well; not Gaelic merely but free as well.

Ibid.

This is a place of peace sacred to the dead where men should speak with all charity and with all restraint; but I hold it a Christian thing, as O'Donovan Rossa held it, to hate evil, to hate untruth, to hate oppression and hating them to strive to overthrow them.

Ibid.

Life springs from death and from the graves of patriot men and women spring living nations. The Defenders of this Realm have worked well in secret and in the open. They think that they have pacified Ireland. They think that they have purchased half of us and intimidated the other half. They think that they have foreseen everything, think they have provided against everything; but the fools, the fools, the fools, they have left us our Fenian dead, and while Ireland holds these graves Ireland unfree shall never be at peace.

Ibid.

Is amhlaigh atá Gaeil na haimsire seo agus a bhformhór ceannaithe ag Gaill. Ní eol dóibh gur amhlaigh atá ach sea. Táid tar éis a ndíolta féin ar ór agus ar airgead nó ar luach óir agus airgid. Tá an fear saibhir tar éis é féin a dhíol ar mhórán agus tá an fear daibhir tar éis é féin a dhíol ar bheagán.

Prímobhalt i 'An Barr Buadh', 16 Márta, 1912.

Tá drong bheag de Ghaeil nach bhfuil ceannaithe fós agus is chucu sin atáimid. An slabhra úd ar ar thráchtamar is féidir é a bhriseadh. BRISTEAR ÓR LE IARANN. Ró-mhinic dár dtaoisigh ag moladh síochána.

Ibid.

17

Tá Éire i gcontúirt a díolta. Ní hé sin amháin é. Tá sí i gcontúirt a díolta agus gan aon dearbhú againn go n-íocfar an luach airgid ar a bhfuiltear dá díol. 'Ná caithigh chun na conairte mé', dúirt Parnell le Gaeil, 'go bhfuighidh sibh an luach airgid ara bhfuil sibh dom dhíol.' Níor éisteadh leis. Caitheadh chun na conairte é agus stracadh óna chéile é. Is mairg do ghní an t-olc agus bhíos bocht ina dhiaidh. Ach dá uafásaí an choir an rinne Gaeil an t-am sin is baolach dóibh coir níos uafásaí a dhéanamh anois. Dhíoladar a gcara an uair sin mar chomaoin ar a namhad. Is é a n-anam féin atá ar an margadh den dul seo agus cuid acu réidh chum a dhíolta ar gheall nach bhfuil aon dearbhú acu go gcóilíonfar go deo é.

Príomhalt i 'An Barr Buadh', 23 Márta, 1912.

Is amhlaigh atá ár dtaoisigh faoi láthair agus drochmhuinín acu as Gaeil agus a seasamh ar Ghaill. Ní maith leo Gaeil dá gcomhairliú ach fulaingid Gaill dá ndalladh. Tá dream díobh agus iad ar a nglúine roimh Ghaill.

Príomh Alt i 'An Barr Buadh', 30 Márta, 1912.

Cad chuige do Wolfe Tone ag éirí i gcoinne na Feise sin? Ár bhfreagra: BHÍ AN FHEIS SIN FAOI CHEANNAS GALL. An bhfuil Gaeil na haoise seo chomh meata sin is go gcuirfidís iad féin faoi gheasa agus faoi mionna bheith dílis do choróin Shasana go deo na ndíleann ach Feis d'fháil a bhéas faoi cheannas Gall agus ceangal i bhfad níos crua uirthi ná mar a bhí ar an bhFeis ar éirigh Wolfe Tone ina coinne? An é atá uainn an ní ná fhulaingeodh Wolfe Tone, ceannas Gall, do bhuanú in Éirinn?

Príomh Alt in 'An Barr Buadh', 6 Aibreán, 1912.

Dá gcaillfí an Ghaeilge chaillfí Éire.

Príomh Alt i 'An Barr Buadh', 4 Bealtaine, 1912.

B'iad na fir óga crann seasta gach cúise dár ghabh Gaeil do láimh a chosaint anuas go dtí ár ré agus ár lá féin. Is iontach a bhfuil de fheara óga ar réim laochra Gael. Ní raibh slán ag Seán an Díomais an uair ar imreadh bás air ach chúig bliana déag is fiche. Níor mhair Aodh Rua Ó Domhnaill ach naoi mbliana fichead. Cúig bliana déag ar fhichead an ré saoil a fuair an fear is fearr dár gineadh riamh de Ghaeil nó de Ghall-Ghaeil in Eirinn, Tiobóid Wolfe Tone. Ceithre bliana is fiche a bhí slán ag Riobeárd Emmet. Ní gá dúinn trácht ar Thomás Dáibhís ná ar an Athair Eoghan Ó Gramhna. Cad as ar fháscumhacht Chonnradh na Talún? As cumhacht croí na n-óg-fhear a bhí ina cheannas. Cad as ar fhás brí agus neart Chonnradh na Gaeilge? As brí agus neart intinne na n-ógfhear a chur ar bun é.

Príomhalt i 'An Barr Buadh', 11 Bealtaine, 1912.

Ní raibh de thaoiseach ná de threoraí ag Gaeil riamh ó theacht do na Normánaigh fear a b'inchurtha le Wolfe Tone ach Aodh Ó Néill. Ach ba mhó d'fhear Wolfe Tone ná Aodh Ó Néill. Ba fhírinní d'fhear é. Ba glaine d'fhear é. Ba neartmhaire d'fhear é. Neart, glaine agus fírinne trí bua an tsárlaoich. 'Neart inár lámha, fírinne ar ár dteanga agus glaine inár gcroí'. Agus ba uafar í doimhneacht intleachta Wolfe Tone agus ba iontach í géire a intinne. Thuig sé dála Gael agus cúrsaí Gall go hiomlán. Ba é an chéad duine a thuig ina gceart iad. Is é a thug léargas agus solas ar an gcúis sin dá dtáinig ina dhiaidh.

Príomhalt i 'An Barr Buadh', 25 Bealtaine, 1912.

Ba gheal le Gaeil tú tráth de d'shaol. An méid dínn a bhí i d'choinne d'admhaíomar go raibh misneach agat thar fheara Éireann an lá ar sheasais ar dheaslámh Parnell agus gáir na conairte go garg gáifeach ina thimpeall. Bhís i d'fhear óg an tráth sin agus táir i d'fhear meánaosta anois. Ní ionann

misneach don óige agus don aois. Bíonn an óige dána.
Bíonn an aois faiteach. Ach cuimhnigh go bhfuil an gníomh
a chuir Parnell roimhe chum a dhéanta gan déanamh fós
agus gur ortsa atá a dhéanamh. Cuimhnigh gurbh ionúin le
Parnell tusa agus gur ionúin le Gaeil tú de bhrí gur ionúin
leis-sean tú. Cuimhnigh gur i d'lámhsa atá claíomh colg-
dhíreach crua Parnell agus gur umatsa atá brat uasal ríoga
Parnell agus gur tusa comharba Parnell. Cuimhnigh go
bhfuil Gaeil ar do chúl. Cuimhnigh go bhfuil Gaill ar
t-aghaidh. Cuimhnigh go bhfuil Gaeil ag seasamh ort.
Cuimhnigh go bhfuil Gaill ag faire ort. Cuimhnigh ar chlú
do chine. Cuimhnigh ar ghliocas do namhad. Cuimhnigh ar
an ní úd dá dtug Parnell fuath agus seachain ar t-anam agus
ar t-oineach í, gáire Sasanaigh. Gabh chugat láidreacht an
leomhain agus misneach an mhathúin agus gliocas na nath-
rach nimhe. Bí borb le borb. Bí teannle teann. Bí crua le
crua. Bí glic le glic. Bí i d'eolach aibidh. Bí i d'choinnil
ghaile. Bí i d'fhear. Bí i d'thaoiseach. Bí i d'Parnell.

Beart Litreach a Chuaigh Amú. 'An Barr Buadh'.
Chun Sheáin Réamuinn. Samhradh, 1912.

Táir rodhorcha ionat féin, a Phiarsaigh. Ní dheánann tú
caidreamh le Gaeil. Séanann tú a gcomhluadar. An uair a
thagas tú ina measc tagann mar a bheadh néall dubh i
d'fhochair agus luíonn orthu. An té a bhí cainteach roimh
teacht duit bíonn sé ina thost. An té a bhí gealgháireach
tagann gruaim air. An í an fhuil Shasanach úd ionat is
ciontach le sin, n'fheadar? Tá bua na cainte agat. Is féidir
leat na sluaite a mhúscailt agus a chorraí an uair labhras tú
leo os ard. Is féidir leat iad a chur ag gol nó iad a chur ag
gáire de réir mar is mian leat. Is dóigh liom go bhfuil dhá
Phiarsach ann, fear gruama doineanta agus fear geal
soineanta. Ní feictear an fear geal soineanta ach go hannamh.
Ar árdáin phoiblí agus i Scoil Éanna is minicí a chítear é.
Bíonn an fear gruama doineanta le feiscint go minic. Is olc

20

an saghas é. Ní maith liom é. Tagann fuacht orm an uair chím é. Agus is í an chud is greannmhaire den scéal nach eol dom céacu an fear dorcha nó an fear geal an Piarsach ceart.

Beart Litreach a Chuaigh Amú. 'An Barr Buadh',
'Chun Phádraic Mhic Phiarais'. Samhradh, 1912.

A French writer has paid the English a very well-deserved compliment. He says that they never commit a useless crime. When they hire a man to assassinate an Irish patriot, when they blow a Sepoy from the mouth of a cannon, when they produce a famine in one of their dependencies they have always an ulterior motive. They do not do it for fun. Humorous as these crimes are it is not the humour of them but their utility that appeals to the English. Unlike Gilbert's Mikado they would see nothing humorous in boiling oil. If they retained boiling oil in their penal code they would retain it as they retain flogging before execution in Egypt, strictly because it has been found useful.

Speech at Mansion House, Dublin, 11 December, 1912.
Published as a pamphlet 'The Murder Machine', 1916.

One is able to form some idea of what distant horizons have been scanned by Irish-speaking men, what heights scaled, what depths sounded. And when our knowledge is just a little wider and deeper than it is at present it will be found that an amazing thing has happened. It will be found that the literary history of the world, what is commonly accepted as literary history, has left out of account one of the great literary peoples. Just as the rediscovery of the buried cities of the East has made it necessary for us to re-write social and political history, so will the discovery of this buried literature of the West make it necessary for us to rewrite literary history. And it will mean not only a re-writing of literary history but a general readjustment of

21

literary values, a general raising of literary standards. The world has had a richer dream of beauty than we had dreamed it had. Men here saw certain gracious things more clearly and felt certain mystic things more acutely and heard certain deep music more perfectly than did men in ancient Greece. And it is from Greece that we have received our standards.

Some Aspects of Irish Literature. A lecture to the
National Literary Society, 9 December, 1912.

How curiously might one speculate if one were to imagine that when the delvers of the fifteenth century unearthed the buried literature of Greece and Rome they had stumbled instead upon that other buried literature which was to remain in the dust of the libraries for four centuries longer! Then instead of the classic revival we should have had the Celtic revival; or rather the Celtic would have become the classic and the Gael would have given laws to Europe. I do not say positively that literature would have gained, but I am not sure that it would have lost. Something it would have lost: the Greek ideal of perfection in form, the wise calm Greek scrutiny. Yes something it would have gained: a more piercing vision, a nobler because a more humane inspiration, above all a deeper spirituality. One other result would have followed: the goodly culture and the fine mysticism of the Middle Ages would not have so utterly been lost. And thinking of the effect of literature upon men's lives and conduct one may add that the world might not have proved so untrue to so many of its righteous causes.

Ibid.

Now I claim for Irish literature at its best these excellences: a clearer than Greek vision, a more generous than Greek humanity, a deeper than Greek spirituality. And I claim

22

that Irish literature has never lost those excellences: that they are of the essence of Irish nature and are characteristic of modern Irish folk poetry even as they are of ancient Irish epic and of mediaeval Irish hymns.

Ibid.

No great literature has shown a subtler understanding of women than Irish literature. Alike in the Táin and in the fugitive songs of the manuscripts and of the countryside we come upon profound intuitions or flashes of imagination which reveal more than many modern novels and much modern poetry. Some of the passages I have quoted will stand as illustrations. And take the couplet of a peasant cradle song which Mr Yeats has elaborated into a charming little lullaby. A mother says to her child:

> Cad déanfaidh mé gan mo ghiolla beag,
> Nuair bheidh tú mór is críonna?

> What shall I do without my little lad
> when you will be big and grown?

Or, as Mr Yeats has it:

> I kiss you and kiss you,
> My pigeon, my own;
> Ah! how I shall miss you,
> When you have grown.

There is a real poignancy there which one does not often meet with in poems of motherhood and childhood. Many mothers must have thought just like that: only a great poet could have imagined it.

Ibid.

I have spoken of the Irish power of clear vivid unadorned statement. Some of you, remembering the rich and royal redundance of a good deal of later Irish verse, will ask whether clear vivid unadorned statement is really an Irish characteristic. It is. It was an Irish characteristic from the beginning and remained an Irish characteristic as long as *Dán Díreach* verse ruled, and longer; for it remains a characteristic of the best of the peasant poetry. The reserve and severity of the early Irish 'I am Eve, great Adam's wife' are as apparent in the seventeenth century poem of Keating, 'A bhean lán de stuaim':

> O woman full of subtlety,
> Keep from me thy hand.

The strength and brevity of the language here are as striking as the candour and energy of the thought. Yet Keating was one of those who ushered in the new school in poetry.

Ibid.

There is no such thing as sentimentality in Irish literature. One finds in later literature, especially in the later poetry, bad taste of various kinds but never that particular kind of bad taste.

Ibid.

There is a place for symbols in literature, but there can be no excuse for using symbols in which you do not yourself believe. That way lies insincerity and without sincerity there can be no literature. Let me illustrate what I mean by a parallel thing which has taken place in recent Anglo-Irish poetry. Either Mr Russell or Mr Yeats discovered a certain symbolism in certain white birds spoken of in connection with Angus in one particular passage of early Irish literature. They straightaway let loose those birds upon Anglo-Irish poetry, and for many of us since the music of Anglo-Irish poetry has almost been drowned by the needless flapping of those white wings. You never open a new book of Anglo-Irish verse but the birds of Angus fly out. It almost reminds one of the nursery rhyme: 'When the pie was opened the birds began to sing.' When the book is opened the birds begin to fly. And the curious thing to us who know *Irish* literature is that the birds of Angus never trouble us there at all. They are the most unobtrusive fowl imaginable.

Ibid.

And it is remarkable that the most chivalrous inspiration in modern literature does in fact come from a Celtic source: that King Arthur and the Knights of the Round Table have meant more to modern man than the heroes who warred at Troy or than Charlemagne and his Paladins. But how much richer might European literature have been had the story of Cúchulainn become a European possession! For the story of Cúchulainn I take to be the finest epic stuff in the world: as we have it, it is not the most finely finished epic, but it is I repeat the finest epic stuff. I mean not merely that Conor and Fergus and Conall and Cúchulainn are nobler figures, humaner figures than Agammemnon and Hector and Ulysses and Achilles; not merely that Macha and Meadhbh and Deirdre and Emer are more gracious figures, more appealing figures, than Hecube and Helen; I mean also that the story itself is greater than any Greek story, the tragedy as pitiful as any Greek tragedy, yet at the same time more joyous, more exultant. The theme is as great as Milton's in 'Paradise Lost': Milton's theme is a fall but the Irish theme is a redemption. For the story of Cúchulainn symbolises the redemption of man by a sinless God. The curse of primal sin lies upon a people; new and personal sin brings doom to their doors; they are powerless to save themselves; a youth free from the curse, akin with them through his mother but through his father divine, redeems them by his valour; and his own death comes from it. I do not mean that the Táin is a conscious allegory: but there is the story in its essence, and it is like a re-telling (or is it a fore-telling?) of the story of Calvary. Whether you agree with me or not, you will agree as to the greatness of the theme stated thus in its essentials; and you will no longer I hope think of the Táin as the tale of an ancient Cattle Drive.

Ibid.

As Mr Colum has pointed out Christ and Mary have been incorporated into the Gaelic clan; and Irish peasant women can keep Christ dead with as real a grief as they keep their own dead. I have many times seen women sob as they repeated or listened to 'The Keening of Mary'. The strange intimacy that connects certain places in Ireland with the scenes of Christ's birth and life and death, and links certain Irish saints and heroes with the joy of the Nativity and the tragedy of the Passion—this is the true Irish mysticism, the mysticism which recognises no real dividing line between the seen and the unseen, and to which the imagined experience is often more vivid than the real experience. A people so gifted must bring in their turn a very precious gift to literature; for is it not the function of literature by making known the real and imagined experiences of gifted souls to reveal to common men all the hidden splendours of the world and to make vocal its silent music?

Ibid.

We of Na Fianna Éireann at the beginning of this year 1914, a year which is likely to be momentous in the history of our country, address ourselves to the boys of Ireland and invite them to band themselves with us in a knightly service. We believe that the highest thing anyone can do is to *serve* well and truly and we purpose to serve Ireland with all our fealty and with all our strength. Two occasions are spoken of in ancient Ireland upon which Irish boys marched to the rescue of their country when it was sore beset—once when Cúchulainn and the boytroop of Ulster held the frontier until the Ulster heroes rose, and again when the boys of Ireland kept the foreign invaders in check on the shores of Ventry until Fionn had rallied the Fianna: it may be that a similar tale shall be told of us and that when men come to write the history of the freeing of Ireland they shall have to record that the boys of Na Fianna Éireann stood in the battle gap until the Volunteers armed.

To the Boys of Ireland. February, 1914.

The object of Na Fianna Éireann is to train the boys of Ireland to fight Ireland's battle when they are men. In the past the Irish, heroicly though they have struggled, have always lost for want of discipline, for want of military knowledge, for want of plans, for want of leaders. The brave Irish who rose in '98, in '48 and in '67 went down because they were not *soldiers*: we hope to train Irish boys from their earliest years to be soldiers, not only to know the trade of a soldier —drilling, marching, camping, signalling, scouting and, when they are old enough, shooting—but also, what is far more important, to understand and prize military discipline and to have a *military spirit*. Centuries of oppression and of unsuccessful effort have almost extinguished the military spirit of Ireland: and if that were once gone—if Ireland were to become a land of contented slaves—it would be very hard, perhaps impossible, to arouse her again.

Ibid.

We believe that Na Fianna Éireann have kept the military spirit alive in Ireland during the past four years and that if the Fianna had not been founded in 1909 the Volunteers of 1913 would never have arisen. In a sense then the Fianna have been the pioneers of the Volunteers; and it is from the ranks of the Fianna that the Volunteers must be recruited. This is a special reason why we should be active during 1914. The Fianna will constitute what the old Irish called the macra or boy-troop of the Volunteers and will correspond to what is called in France an Ecole Polytechnique or Military School. As the man who was to lead the armies of France to such glorious victories came forth from the Military School of Brienne, so may the man who shall lead the Irish Volunteers to victory come forth from Na Fianna Éireann.

Ibid.

Finally, we believe with Thomas Davis that 'righteous men' must 'make our land a Nation Once Again'. Hence we endeavour to train our boys to be pure, truthful, honest, sober, kindly; clean in heart as well as in body; generous in their service to their parents and companions now as we would have them generous in their service to their country hereafter. We bear a very noble name and inherit very noble traditions for we are called after the Fianna of Fionn, that heroic companionship which, according to legend, flourished in Ireland in the second and third centuries of the Christian era.

> We, the Fianna, never told a lie,
> Falsehood was never imputed to us,

said Oisín to Saint Patrick; and again when Patrick asked Caoilte Mac Rónáin how it came that the Fianna won all their battles, Caoilte replied: 'Strength that was in our hands, truth that was on our lips, and purity that was in our breasts.'

Ibid.

Is it too much to hope that after so many centuries the old ideals are still quick in the heart of Irish youth and that this year we shall get many hundred Irish boys to come forward and help us to build up a brotherhood of young Irishmen strong of limb, true and pure in tongue and heart, chivalrous, cultured in a really Irish sense, and ready to spend themselves in the service of their country?

Ibid.

We want recruits because we have undertaken a service which we believe to be of vital importance to our country, and because that service needs whatever there is of manly stuff of Ireland in order to its effective rendering.

Why We Want Recruits. May, 1915.

We want recruits because we have a standard to rally them to. It is not a new standard raised for the first time by the men of a new generation. It is an old standard which has been borne by many generations of Irish men, which has gone into many battles, which has looked down upon much glory and upon much sorrow; which has been a sign to be contradicted but which shall yet shine as a star. There is no other standard in the world so august as the standard we bear; and it is the only standard which the men of Ireland may bear without abandoning their ancient allegiance. Individual Irishmen have sometimes fought under other standards: Ireland as a whole has never fought under any other.

Ibid.

We want recruits because we have a faith to give them and a hope with which to inspire them. They are a faith and a hope which have been handed down from generation to generation of Irish men and women unto this last. The faith is that Ireland is one, that Ireland is inviolate, that Ireland is worthy of all love and all homage and all service that may lawfully be paid to any earthly thing; and the hope is that Ireland may be free. In a human sense we have no desire, no ambition but the integrity, the honour and the freedom of our native land.

Ibid.

We want recruits because we are sure of the rightness of our cause. We have no misgivings, no self-questionings. While others have been doubting, timorous, ill at ease, we have been serenely at peace with our consciences. The recent time of soul-searching had no terrors for us. We saw our path with absolute clearness; we took it with absolute deliberateness. 'We could no other.' We called upon the names of the great confessors of our national faith and all was well with us. Whatever soul-searchings there may be among Irish political parties now or hereafter, we go on in the calm certitude of having done the clear, clean, sheer thing. We have the strength and the peace of mind of those who never compromise.

Ibid.

We want recruits because we believe that events are about to place the destinies of Ireland definitely in our hands and because we want as much help as possible to enable us to bear the burden. The political leadership of Ireland is passing to us—not, perhaps, to us as individuals for none of us is ambitious for leadership and few of us fit for leadership; but to our party, to men of our way of thinking: that is to the party and to the men that stand by the nation, to the party and to the men of one allegiance.

Ibid.

We want recruits because we have work for them to do. We do not propose to keep our men idle. We propose to give them work, hard work, plenty of work. We would band together all men capable of working for Ireland and give them men's work.

Ibid.

We want recruits because we are able to train them. The great majority of our officers are now fully competent to undertake the training of Irish Volunteers for active service under the conditions imposed by the natural and military facts of the map of Ireland. Those officers who are not so competent will be made competent in our training camps during the next few months.

Ibid.

We want recruits because we are able to arm them. In a rough way of speaking we have succeeded already in placing a gun and ammunition therefore in the hands of every Irish Volunteer that has undertaken to endeavour to pay for them. We are in a position to do as much for every man that joins us. We may not always have the popular pattern of gun, but we undertake to produce a gun of some sort for every genuine Irish Volunteer; with some ammunition to boot.

Ibid.

We want recruits because we are absolutely determined to take action the moment action becomes a duty. If a moment comes—as a moment seemed on the point of coming at least twice during the past eighteen months—when the Irish Volunteers will be justified to their consciences in taking definite military action, such action will be taken. We do not anticipate such a moment in the very near future; but we live at a time when it may come swiftly and terribly. What if Conscription be forced upon Ireland? What if a Unionist or Coalition British Ministry repudiate the Home Rule Act? What if it be determined to dismember Ireland? What if it be attempted to disarm Ireland? The future is big with these and other possibilities.

Ibid.

Always it is the many who fight for the evil thing and the few who fight for the good thing; and always it is the few who win. For God fights with the small battalions. If sometimes it has seemed otherwise it is because the few who have fought for the good cause have been guilty of some secret faltering, some infidelity to their best selves, some shrinking back in the face of a tremendous duty.

Peace and the Gael. December, 1915.

War is a terrible thing but war is not an evil thing. It is the things that make war necessary that are evil. The tyrannies that wars break, the lying formulae that wars overthrow, the hypocrisies that wars strip naked are evil.

Ibid.

It is because peace is so precious a boon that war is so sacred a duty. Ireland will not find Christ's peace until she has taken Christ's sword. What peace she has known in these latter days has been the devil's peace, peace with sin, peace with dishonour. It is a foul thing, dear only to men of foul breeds. Christ's peace is so lovely in its coming, beautiful are its feet on the mountains. But it is heralded by terrific messengers; seraphim and cherubim blow trumpets of war before it. We must not flinch when we are passing through that uproar; we must not faint at the sight of blood. Winning through it we (or those of us who survive) shall come unto great joy. We and our fathers have known the Pax Britannica. To our sons we must bequeath the Peace of the Gael.

Ibid.

Some of my friends have been looking forward to my story of how Scoil Éanna came to be. There is very little to tell. Various high and patriotic motives have been assigned to me in the press and elsewhere. I am conscious of one motive only namely a love of boys, of their ways, of their society; and a desire to help as many boys as possible to become good men. To me a boy is the most interesting of all living things, and I have for years found myself coveting the privilege of being in a position to mould or help to mould the lives of boys to noble ends. In my sphere as a journalist and University teacher no opportunity for the exercise of such a privilege existed; finally I decided to create my opportunity. I interested a few friends in the project of a school which should aim at the making of good men rather than of learned men, but of men truly learned rather than of persons qualified to pass examinations; and as my definition of a good man, as applied to an Irishman, includes his being a good Irishman (for you cannot make an Irish boy a good Englishman or a good Frenchman), and as my definition of learning as applied to an Irishman includes Irish learning as its basis and fundament, it followed that my school should be an Irish school in a sense not known or dreamt of in Ireland since the Flight of the Earls. This project, I say, appealed to two or three friends whose hearts were pat with mine; and Scoil Éanna is the result.

The Story of a Success. June, 1909.

In no other school in Ireland can there be in proportion to its size so much of the stuff out of which men and nations are made. There is hardly a boy of all our seventy who does not come from a home which has traditions of work and sacrifice for Ireland, traditions of literary, scholarly or political service. If every boy in the Boy-Corps of Eamhain Macha was the son of a hero nearly every boy in the Boy-Corps of Scoil Éanna is the son or brother or cousin of some man or woman who is graving a mark in the history of contemporary Ireland. That in itself is a very splendid inspiration. It is much for a boy to start life with the conscious knowledge: 'I am the son of a good father.'

Ibid.

We must be worthy of our fame as the most Irish of Irish schools. We must be worthy of Ireland. We must be worthy of the men and women whose names we bear. We must be worthy of the tradition we seek to recreate and perpetuate in Éire, the knightly tradition of the macradh of Eamhain Mhacha, dead at the Ford 'in the beauty of their boyhood', the high tradition of Cúchulainn, 'better is short life with honour than long life with dishonour', 'I care not though I were to live but one day and one night if only my fame and my deeds live after me'; the noble tradition of the Fianna, 'we, the Fianna, never told a lie, falsehood was never imputed to us', 'strength in our hands, truth on our lips and cleanness in our hearts'; the Christlike tradition of Colm Cille, 'if I die, it shall be from excess of the love I bear the Gael'. It seems to me that with this appeal it will be an easy thing to teach Irish boys to be brave and unselfish, truthful and pure; I am certain that no other appeal will so stir their hearts or kindle their imagination to heroic things.

Ibid.

The value of the national factor in education would appear to rest chiefly in this, that it addresses itself to the most generous side of the child's nature urging him to live up to his finest self. I think that the true work of the teacher may be said to be to induce the child to realise himself at his best and worthiest, and if this be so the factor of nationality is of prime importance apart from any ulterior propagandist view the teacher may cherish. Even if I were not a Gaelic Leaguer committed to the service of a cause it would still be my duty, from a purely pedagogic point of view, to make my school as Irish as a school can possibly be made.

Ibid.

What I mean by an Irish school is a school that takes Ireland for granted.

Ibid.

You need not praise the Irish language—simply speak it; you need not denounce English games—play Irish ones; you need not ignore foreign history, foreign literature—deal with them from the Irish point of view. An Irish school need no more be a purely Irish-speaking school than an Irish nation need be a purely Irish-speaking nation; but an Irish school, like an Irish nation, must be permeated through and through by Irish culture, the repository of which is the Irish language.

Ibid.

I do not think that a purely Irish-speaking school is a thing to be desired; at all events a purely Irish-speaking secondary or higher school is a thing that is no longer possible. Secondary education in these days surely implies the adding of some new culture, that is of some new language with its

35

literature to the culture enshrined in the mother tongue; and the proper teaching of a new language always invokes a certain amount of bilingualism—unless indeed we are to be content with construing from the new language into our own, a very poor accomplishment. The new language ought to become in some sense a second vernacular; so that it is not sufficient to speak it during the limited portion of the school-day that can be devoted to its teaching as a specific subject; it must be introduced during the ordinary work of the school, as a teaching medium, side by side with the original vernacular. This argument justifies bilingualism as an educational resource, always and everywhere; but in Ireland where there are already two living vernaculars, bilingualism is an educational necessity. Obviously too it is the one irresistible engine at the disposal of those who would restore Irish as a living medium of speech to the non-Irish-speaking three-fourths of the country.

Ibid.

To be concrete, at Scoil Éanna every child is taught Irish. Of thirty in the Infants and Junior Division only one child uses Irish as a vernacular so that English is necessarily the basis of the elementary instruction; but Irish has been taught even to the youngest mites since the first day the School opened, is used freely in the school-room and is cautiously employed in giving instruction in such subjects as Arithmetic, Nature-Study and Physical Drill. In the Senior School the instruction throughout (with the exception of that in Higher Mathematics and Mathematical Science where English must necessarily predominate until we have Irish text-books and a recognised body of technical terms) is fully bilingual. That is to say Irish, English and other modern languages are taught, each through the medium both of Irish and English. As regards procedure, occasionally a lesson is given in Irish only or in English

36

only; but the rule is whether the subject be Christian Doctrine or Algebra, Nature-Study or Latin, to teach the lesson first in Irish and then repeat it in English or vice-versa. In such subjects as Dancing and Physical Drill English can practically be dispensed with. As a general medium of communication between masters and pupils in the schoolroom Irish is the more commonly used of the two vernaculars.

Ibid.

Philosophy is as old as the hills and the science of today is only a new flowering of the science that made lovely the ancient cities and gardens of the east. With all our learning we are not yet as cultured as were the Greeks who crowded to hear the play of Sophocles; with all our art institutions we have not yet that love for the beautiful which burned in the heart of the middle ages.

The Story of a Success. Strivings. December, 1909.

All the problems with which we strive were long ago solved by our ancestors, only their solutions have been forgotten. Take the problem of education, that is the problem of bringing up a child. We constantly speak and write as if a philosophy of education were first formulated in our own time. But all the wise peoples of old faced and solved that problem for themselves and most of their solutions were better than ours. Professor Culverwell thinks that the Jews gave it the best solution. For my part I salute the old Irish. The philosophy of education is preached now but is was practised by the founders of the Gaelic system two thousand years ago. Their very names for 'education' and 'teacher' and 'pupil' show that they had gripped the heart of the problem. The word for 'education' among the old Gael was the same as the word for 'fostering'; the teacher was a 'fosterer' and the pupil was a 'foster-child'. Now to

37

'foster' is exactly the function of a teacher: not primarily
to 'lead up', to 'guide', to 'conduct through a course of
studies', and still less to 'indoctrinate', to 'inform', to
'prepare for exams', but primarily to 'foster' the elements
of character already present.

Ibid.

One does not want to make each of one's pupils a replica
of oneself (Gof forbid), holding the selfsame opinions, pre-
judices, likes, illusions. Neither does one want to drill all
one's pupils into so many regulation little soldiers or so
many stodgy little citizens, though this is apparently the
aim of some of the most cried-up of modern systems.

Ibid.

In point of fact man is not primarily a member of a State
but a human individuality—that is a human soul imprison-
ed in a human body; a shivering human soul with its own
awful problems, its own august destiny, lonelier in its house
of clay than any prisoner in any Bastille in the world.

Ibid.

The true teacher will recgonise in each of his pupils an
individual human soul, distinct and different from every
other human soul that has ever been fashioned by God,
miles and miles apart from the soul that is nearest and most
akin to it, craving indeed comradeship and sympathy and
pity, needing also, it may be, discipline and guidance and a
restraining hand, but imperiously demanding to be allowed
to live its own life, to be allowed to bring itself to its own
perfection; because for every soul there is a perfection
meant for it alone, and which it alone is capable of attain-
ing. So the primary office of the teacher is to 'foster' that

of good which is native to the soul of his pupil, striving to bring its inborn excellences to ripeness rather than to implant in it excellences exotic to its nature. It comes to this then that the education of a child is greatly a matter in the first place of congenial environment and next to this of a wise and loving watchfulness whose chief appeal will be to the finest instincts of the child itself.

Ibid.

It is a long time since I was first attracted by the Gaelic plan of educating children. One of my oldest recollections is of a kindly grey-haired seanchaí, a woman of my mother's people, telling tales by the kitchen fireplace. She spoke more wisely and nobly of ancient heroic things than anyone else I have ever known. Her only object was to amuse me, yet she was the truest of all my teachers. One of her tales was of a king, the most famous king of his time in Ireland, who had gathered about him a number of boys, the children of his friends and kinsmen, whom he had organised into a little society giving them a constitution and allowing them to make their own laws and elect their own leaders. The most renowned of the king's heroes was appointed to teach them chivalry, the most skilled of his men of art to teach them arts, the wisest of his druids to teach them philosophy. The king himself was one of their teachers and so did he love their companionship that he devoted one third of all the time he saved from affairs of state to teaching them or watching them at play; and if any stranger came to the dún during that time, even though he were a king's envoy demanding audience, there was but one answer to him: 'the king is with his foster-children'. This was my first glimpse of the Boy-Corps of Eamhain Mhacha and the picture has remained in my heart.

Ibid.

In truth, I think that the old Irish plan of education as idealised for boys in the story of the Macradh of Eamhain and for girls in that of the Grianán of Lusga was the wisest and most generous that the world has ever known. The bringing together of children in some pleasant place under the fosterage of some man famous among his people for his greatness of heart, for his wisdom, for his skill in some gracious craft—here we get the two things on which I lay most stress in education, the environment, and the stimulus of a personality which can address itself to the child's worthiest self.

Ibid.

As the Boy-Corps of Eamhain stands out as the idealisation of the system Cúchulainn stands out as the idealisation of the child fostered under the system. And thus Cúchulainn describes his fostering: 'Fionnchaomh nourished me at her breast; Feargus bore me on his knee; Conall was my companion-in-arms; Blai, the lord of lands, was my hospitaller; fair-speeched Seancha trained me in just judgment; on the knee of Amhairgin the poet I learned poetry; Cathbhadh of the gentle face taught me druid lore; Conchobar kindled my boyish ambition. All the chariot-chiefs and kings and poets of Ulster have taken part in my bringing-up.' Such was the education of Cúchulainn, the most perfect hero of the Gael.

Ibid.

Cúchulainn may never have lived and there may never have been a Boy-Corps at Eamhain; but the picture endures as the Gael's idealisation of the kind of environment and the kind of fostering which go to the making of a perfect hero. The result of it all, the simplicity and the strength of true heroism, is compressed into a single sentence put into the mouth of the hero by the old shaper of the tale of Cúchulainn's Phantom Chariot: 'I was a child with children; I was a man with men.'

Ibid.

Civilisation has taken such a queer turn that it might not be easy to restore the old Irish plan of education in all its details. Our heroes and seers and scholars would not be so willing to add a Boy-Corps or a Grianán to their establishments as were their prototypes in Ireland from time immemorial till the fall of the Gaelic polity. I can imagine how blue Dr Hyde, Mr Yeats and Mr MacNeill would look if their friends informed them that they were about to send their children to be fostered.

But at least we can bring the heroes and seers and scholars to the schools (as we do at Scoil Éanna) and get them to talk to the children; and we can rise up against the system which tolerates as teachers the rejected of all other professions, rather than demanding for so priestlike an office the highest souls and the noblest intellects of the race.

Ibid.

In pleading for an attractive school-life I do not plead for making school-life one long grand picnic: I have no sympathy with sentimentalists who hold that we should surround children with an artificial happiness, shutting out from their ken pain and sorrow and retribution and the world's law of unending strife; the key-note of the school-life I desiderate is effort on the part of the child itself, struggle, self-sacrifice, self-discipline for by these only does the soul rise to perfection. I believe in gentleness but not in softness. I would not place too heavy a burden on young shoulders, but I would see that no one, boy or man, shirk the burden he is strong enough to bear.

Ibid.

I do not know that any man ought to make himself responsible for the education of multitudes of children; at any rate to get to know a hundred and fifty boys as a master ought to know his pupils is a task that I feel sufficiently big for myself at present. The work is fascinating. One's life in a school is a perpetual adventure, an adventure among souls and minds; each child is a mystery and if the plucking out of the heart of so many mysteries is fraught with much labour and anxiety there are compensations richer than have ever rewarded any voyagers among treasure islands in tropic seas.

Ibid.

Nothing has given me greater pleasure during the past session than to watch Scoil Éanna developing as it has been doing on the athletic side. Our boys must now be amongst the best hurlers and footballers in Ireland. Wellington is credited with the dictum that the battle of Waterloo was won on the playing fields of Eaton. I am certain that when it comes to a question of Ireland winning battles her main reliance must be on her hurlers. To your camáns, O boys of Banba.

Ibid.

In most of the enterprises of life a fund of faith is a more valuable asset than a sum in Consols. Many years ago I knew a parish priest who wanted to build a church. He went to his bank for a loan. When asked by the bank manager what security he had to offer he made the simple and natural reply: 'St Joseph will see you paid.' 'St Joseph is an estimable saint,' said the bank manager, 'but unfortunately he is not a negotiable security.' The *mot* passed into a proverb among the commercial folk of Dublin and the bank manager gained the reputation of a wit. Both bank manager and priest have since gone down to dusty death; but the priest's dying eyes saw his church walls rising slowly and today the church stands grave and beautiful in the midst of the people. The laugh, to speak without irreverance, is on the side of St Joseph. So does the spiritual always triumph over the actual (for the spiritual being the true actual is stronger than the forms and bulks we call actual) and a simple man's faith is found more potent than a negotiable instrument.

The Story of a Success. Adventures. Christmas 1910.

My friends and I hope and believe that we have found in Scoil Éanna and Scoil Íde two noble schools which for many years to come will send out Irish boys and girls filled with that heroic spirit which in old days gave Macha strength to run her race and prompted Enda to leave a king's house for the desolation of Aran and which in the days of our great-grandfathers sent Emmet with a smiling face to the gibbet in Thomas Street and nerved Anne Devlin to bare her back to the scourges of Sirr's soldiery. A new heroic age in Ireland may be a visionary's dream or it may come about in some other way than that which we have planned; our schools may pass away or degenerate: but at least this attempt has been made, this right thing has been striven after and there will be something to the good somewhere if it be only a memory and a resolve in the heart of one of the least of our pupils.

Ibid.

I believe that many teachers fail because instead of endeavouring to raise themselves to the level of their pupils (I mean the moral, emotional and imaginative level) they endeavour to bring their pupils down to theirs. For a high if eccentric moral code, a glad and altruistic philosophy, a

43

vision of ultimate beauty and truth seen through the fantastic and often humorous figments of a child's dreams, the teacher substitutes the mean philosophy of the world, the mean code of morals of the countinghouse.

The Story of a Success. Rejoicings. May, 1913.

Our Christianity becomes respectable. We are not content with teaching the Ten Commandments that God spake in thunder and Christ told us to keep if we would enter unto life, and the precepts of the Church which he commanded us to hear: we add thereto the precepts or commandments of Respectable Society. And these are chiefly six: Thou shalt not be extreme in anything—in wrongdoing lest thou be put to gaol, in rightdoing lest thou be deemed a saint; Thou shalt not give away thy substance lest thou become a pauper; Thou shalt not engage in trade or manufacture lest thy hands become grimy; Thou shalt not carry a brown paper parcel lest thou shock Rathgar; Thou shalt not have an enthusiasm lest solicitors and their clerks call thee a fool; Thou shalt not endanger thy job. One has heard this shocking morality taught in Christian schools, expounded in Christian newspapers, even preached from Christian pulpits. These things about the lilies of the field and the birds of the air and that rebuke to Martha who was troubled about many things are thought to have no relevancy to modern life. But if that is so Christianity has no relevancy to modern life for these are the essence of Christ's teaching.

Ibid.

The great enemy of practical Christianity has always been respectable society. Respectable society has now been reinforced by political economy. I feel sure that political economy was invented not by Adam Smith but by the devil. Perhaps Adam Smith was the human instrument of whom that wily one made use even as he made use of the elder Adam to pervert men to the ways of respectability. Be certain that in political economy there is no Way of Life either for a man or for a people. Life for both is a matter not of conflicting tariffs but of conflicting powers of good and evil; and what have Ricardo and Malthus and Stuart Mill to teach about this? Ye men and peoples, burn your books on rent theories and land values and go back to your sagas.

Ibid.

If you will not go back to your sagas your sagas will come to you again in new guise: for they are terrible immortal things, not capable of being put down by respectable society or by political economy. The old truths will find new mouths, the old sorrows and ecstacies new interpretation. Beauty is the garment of truth or perhaps we should put it that beauty is the substance in which truth bodies itself forth; and then we can say that beauty like matter is indestructible; however it may change its form. When you think that you have excluded it by your brick walls it flows in upon you, multitudinous. I know not how the old beauty will come back for us in this country and century; though an Irish theatre perhaps, or through a new poetry swelling up in Irish speaking villages. But come back it will, and its coming will be as the coming of God's angel, when

'. . . seems another morn
Risen on mid-noon. . . '

Ibid.

Mo ghrá sibh, a fheara Éireann, a d'fhreagair an chomh ghairm seo in bhur mílte, ní hea ach in bhur gcéata mílte. Mo ghoirm sibh thar fheara an domhain ar bhur ndílseacht, ar bhur ndóchas, ar bhur ndianchomhrac. A Dhia na bhFeart,

45

nach fada an cogadh againn é! Nár mhór í ár bhfoighid! Nár bhuan é ár misneach! Tá daoine ar an láthair seo gur cuimhin leo ocht agus ceathrú milliún Gael ar thalamh na hÉireann. Níl againne ach ceithre mhilliún agus a dtrian san ceannaithe ag Gaill. Ach ní lúide ár misneach an díth a chuaigh orainn agus ní lúide ár ndóchas na catha a briseadh orainn. Músclaimis ár meanma arís. Tá oiread anseo is a chuirfeadh impireacht Shasana ar neamhní ach iad a bheith ar aon aigne agus iad do chur chuige i gceart.

Óráid i Sráid Ó Conaill, Baile Átha Cliath,
faoi cheannas Sheáin Réamoinn. 31 Márta, 1912.

Níl uainne impireacht Shasana a chur ar neamhní. Céard tá uainn? Tá saoirse Gael. Ní thigimid ar fad le chéile i mion-nithe. Is cuma san. Táimid ar fad ar aon aigne i dtaobh na méide seo—go bhfuil de dhualgas orainn saoirse a bhaint amach dár gcine ar ais nó ar éigean. Tá dream dínn a bheadh sásta le bheith faoi cheannas Rí Shasana ach saoirse a bheith againn inar bhfearainn féin. Tá dream eile dínn nár chrom ár gceann is nár fheac ár nglúin in ómós do Rí Shasana riamh agus nach ndéanfaidh go deo. Táim-se ar an dara dream den dá dhream sin mar is eol do chách.

Ibid.

Ach chítear dom gur amhlaidh bheinn ag déanamh feall ar mo mhuinntir lá curtha an chatha mura bhfreagróinn an chomhghairm seo inniu óir is léir domsa go rachaidh an reacht seo atá dá mholadh dúinn i dtairbhe do Ghaeil agus go mba treise Gaeil chum troda faoin reacht ná ina éagmais. An té atá ar an intinn sin ní bheadh ann ach cladhaire mura dtiúrfadh sé cúnamh chun an reacht a bhaint amach. Ná tuigtear go bhfuilim ag glacadh leis an reacht roimh ré. Níl éinne ag glacadh leis an reacht roimh ré. Bfhéidir go mbeadh orainn diúltú don reacht. Níl dá rá againn inniu ach go gcaifear éisteacht le glór Gael feasta, go bhfuil ár bhfoighid caite.

Ibid.

Tá Gaeil dá fhógairt agus dhá chéad míle díobh ag labhairt anseo d'aitheasc aonduine go bhfuil saoirse uathu agus go bhfuil fúthu a bhaint amach. Cuirimis le chéile agus bainimis racht maith de Ghaill. Is dóigh liom gur féidir reacht maith a bhaint díobh ach ár ndóthain misnigh do ghabháil chugainn. Agus má clistear orainn den dul seo tá dream in Éirinn agus táimse ar dhuine díobh a mholfas do Ghaeil gan dul in gcomhairle nó i gcaidreamh le Gaill go deo arís ach iad a fhreagairt feasta le láimh láidir agus le faobhar claidhimh. Tuigeadh Gaill má fealltar orainn arís go mheidh ina chogadh chraorag ar fud na hÉireann.

Ibid.

THE FOOL

Since the wise men have not spoken, I speak that am only a
    fool;
A fool that hath loved his folly,
Yea, more than the wise men their books or their counting
    houses, or their quiet homes,
Or their fame in men's mouths;
A fool that in all his days hath done never a prudent thing,
Never hath counted the cost, nor recked if another reaped
The fruit of his mighty sowing, content to scatter the seed;
A fool that is unrepentant, and that soon at the end of all
Shall laugh in his lonely heart as the ripe ears fall to the
    reaping-hooks
And the poor are filled that were empty,
Tho' he go hungry.

47

I have squandered the splendid years that the Lord God
      gave to my youth
In attempting impossible things, deeming them alone worth
      the toil.
Was it folly or grace? Not men shall judge me, but God.

I have squandered the splendid years:
Lord, if I had the years I would squander them over again,
Aye, fling them from me!
For this I have heard in my heart, that a man shall scatter,
      not hoard,
Shall do the deed of today, nor take thought of tomorrow's
      teen,
Shall not bargain or huxter with God; or was it a jest of
      Christ's
And is this my sin before me, to have taken him at his word?

The lawyers have sat in council, the men with the keen,
      long faces,
And said, 'This man is a fool,' and others have said, 'He
      blasphemeth';
And the wise have pitied the fool that hath striven to give a
      life
In the world of time and space among the bulks of actual
      things,
To a dream that was dreamed in the heart, and that only
      the heart could hold.

O wise men, riddle me this: what if the dream come true?
What if the dream come true? and if millions unborn shall
      dwell
In the house that I shaped in my heart, the noble house of
      my thought?
Lord, I have staked my soul, I have staked the lives of my
      kin
On the truth of thy dreadful word. Do not remember my
      failures,
But remember this my faith.

And so I speak.
Yea, ere my hot youth pass, I speak to my people and say:
Ye shall be foolish as I; ye shall scatter not save;
Ye shall venture your all, lest ye lose what is more than all;
Ye shall call for a miracle, taking Christ at his word.
And for this I will answer, O people, answer here and here-
        after,
O people that I have loved shall we not answer together?

THE WAYFARER

The beauty of the world hath made me sad,
This beauty that will pass;
Sometimes my heart hath shaken with great joy
To see a leaping squirrel in a tree,
Or a red ladybird upon a stalk,
Or little rabbits in a field at evening,
Lit by a slanting sun,
Or some green hill where shadows drifted by
Some quiet hill where mountainy man hath sown
And soon would reap; near to the gate of heaven;
Or children with bare feet upon the sands
Of some ebbed sea, or playing on the streets
Of little towns in Connacht,
Things young and happy.
And then my heart hath told me:
These will pass,
Will pass and change, will die and be no more,
Things bright and green, things young and happy;
And I have gone upon my way
Sorrowful.

CHRISTMAS

1915

O King that was born
To set bondsmen free,
In the coming battle,
Help the Gael!

THE MOTHER

I do not grudge them: Lord, I do not grudge
My two strong sons that I have seen go out
To break their strength and die, they and a few,
In bloody protest for a glorious thing,
They shall be spoken of among their people,
The generations shall remember them,
And call them blessed;
But I will speak their names to my own heart
In the long nights;
The little names that were familiar once
Round my dead hearth.
Lord, thou art hard on mothers:
We suffer in their coming and their going;
And tho' I grudge them not, I weary, weary
Of the long sorrow — And yet I have my joy:
My sons were faithful, and they fought.

The English administration of Ireland has not been marked
by any unnecessary cruelty. Every crime that the English
have planned and carried out in Ireland has had a definite
end. Every absurdity that they have set up has had a grave
purpose.

The Murder Machine, 1916.

I have spent the greater part of my life in immediate con-
templation of the most grotesque and horrible of the
English inventions for the debasement of Ireland. I mean
their education system.

Ibid.

The education system here was designed by our masters in
order to make us willing or at least manageable slaves. It has
made of some Irishmen not slaves merely but very eunuchs
with the indifference and cruelty of eunuchs; kinless beings
who serve for pay a master that they neither love nor hate.

Ibid.

In particular I would urge that the Irish school system of
the future should give freedom—freedom to the individual
school, freedom to the individual teacher, freedom as far as
may be to the individual pupil. Without freedom there can
be no right growth; and education is properly the fostering
of the right growth of a personality.

Ibid.

Ireland in our day as in the past has excommunicated some
of those who have served her best and has canonised some
of those who have served her worst. We damn a man for an
unpopular phrase; we deify a man who does a mean thing
gracefully.

From a Hermitage. June, 1913.

When a man like Synge, a man in whose sad heart there
glowed a true love of Ireland, one of the two or three men
who have in our time made Ireland considerable in the eyes
of the world, uses strange symbols which we do not under-

stand, we cry out that he has blasphemed and we proceed to crucify him. When a sleek lawyer rising step by step through the most ignoble of all professions attains to a Lord Chancellorship or to an Attorney-Generalship we confer upon him the freedom of our cities.

Ibid.

As long as Ireland is unfree the only honourable attitude for Irishmen and Irishwomen is an attitude of revolt.

From a Hermitage. July, 1913.

I agree with one who holds that John Mitchel is Ireland's greatest literary figure—that is of those who have written in English. But I place Tone above him both as a man and as a leader of men. Tone's was a broader humanity with as immense a nationality; Tone's was a sunnier nature with as stubborn a soul. But Mitchel stands next to Tone: and these two shall teach you and lead you.

From a Hermitage. September, 1913.

My instinct is with the landless man against the lord of lands, and with the breadless man against the master of millions. I may be wrong but I hold it a most terrible sin that there should be landless men in this island of waste yet fertile valleys, and that there should be breadless men in this city where great fortunes are made and enjoyed.

From a Hermitage. October, 1913.

I calculate that one-third of the people of Dublin are underfed; that half the children attending Irish primary schools are ill-nourished. Inspectors of the National Board will tell you that there is no use in visiting primary schools in Ire-

52

land after one or two in the afternoon: the children are too weak and drowsy with hunger to be capable of answering intelligently. I suppose there are twenty thousand families in Dublin in whose domestic economy milk and butter are all but unknown: black tea and dry bread are their stable articles of diet. There are many thousand fireless hearth-places in Dublin on the bitterest days of winter; there would be many thousand more only for such bodies as the Society of St Vincent de Paul. Twenty thousand Dublin families live in one room tenements. It is common to find two or three families occupying the same room; and some-times one of the families will have a lodger! There are tenement rooms in Dublin in which over a dozen persons live, eat and sleep.

From a Hermitage. October, 1913.

I do not know whether the methods of Mr James Larkin are wise methods or unwise methods (unwise, I think, in some respects) but this I know, that here is a most hideous wrong to be righted and that the man who attempts to right it is a good and a brave man.

Ibid.

The Orangeman is ridiculous in so far as he believes incred-ible things; he is estimable in so far as he is willing and able to fight in defence of what he believes. It is foolish of an Orangeman to believe that his personal liberty is threatened by Home Rule; but granting that he believes that, it is not only in the highest degree common sense but it is his clear duty to arm in defence of his threatened liberty.

From a Hermitage. November, 1913.

There were many men of money among the Volunteers of 1778-83: it was one of the weaknesses of the movement. Those who have are always inclined to hold; always afraid to risk. No good cause in Ireland appeals for help in vain provided those to whom it appeals are sufficiently poor.

From a Hermitage. January, 1914.

The leaders in Ireland have nearly always left the people at the critical moment; have sometimes sold them. The former Volunteer movement was abandoned by its leaders; hence its ultimate failure. Grattan 'led the van' of the Volunteers but he also led the retreat of the leaders; O'Connell recoiled before the cannon of Clontarf; twice the hour of the Irish Revolution struck during Young Ireland days and twice it struck in vain, for Meagher hesitated in Waterford, Duffy and McGee hesitated in Dublin. Stephens refused to 'give the word' in '65; he never came in '66 or '67. I do not blame these men: you and I might have done the same.

Ibid.

War is a terrible thing and this is the most terrible of wars. But this war is not more terrible than the evils which it will end or help to end. It is not more terrible than the exploitation of the English masses by cruel plutocrats; it is not more terrible than the infidelity of the French masses to their old spiritual ideals; it is not more terrible than the enslavement of the Poles by Russia, than the enslavement of the Irish by England. What if the war kindles in the slow breasts of English toilers a wrath like the wrath of the French in 1789? What if the war brings France back to her altars as sorrow brings back broken men and women to God? What if the war sets Poland and Ireland free? If the war does those things will not the war have been worthwhile?

'Peace and the Gael', December, 1915.

The men who have led Ireland for twenty-five years have done evil and they are bankrupt. They are bankrupt in policy, bankrupt in credit, bankrupt now even in words. They have nothing to propose to Ireland, no way of wisdom, no counsel of courage. When they speak they speak only untruth and blasphemy. Their utterances are no longer the utterances of men. They are the mumblings and the gibberings of lost souls. One finds oneself wondering what sin these men have been guilty of that so great a shame should come upon them. Is it that they are punished with loss of manhood because in their youth they committed a crime against manhood? ... Does the ghost of Parnell haunt them to their damnation?

'Ghosts', Christmas Day, 1915.

If I do not hold the faith of Tone and if Tone was not a heretic then I am. If Tone said 'Break the connection with England', and if I say 'Maintain the connection with England', I may be preaching a saner (as I am certainly preaching a safer) gospel than his, but I am obviously not preaching the same gospel.

Ibid.

I make the contentions that the national demand of Ireland is fixed and determined; that that demand had been made by every generation; that we of this generation receive it as a trust from our fathers; that we are bound by it; that we have not the right to alter it or to abate it by one jot or tittle; and that any undertaking made in the name of Ireland to accept in full satisfaction of Ireland's claim anything less than the generations of Ireland have stood for is null and void, binding on Ireland neither by the law of God nor by the law of nations.

Ibid.

Ireland's historic claim is for Separation. Ireland has authorised no man to abate that claim. The man who in the name of Ireland accepts as 'a final settlement' anything less by one fraction of an iota than Separation from England will be repudiated by the new generation as surely as O'Connell was repudiated by the generation that came after him. The man who in return for the promise of a thing which is not merely less than Separation, but which denies Separation and proclaims the Union perpetual, the man who in return for this declares peace between Ireland and England and sacrifices to England as a peace-holocaust the blood of fifty thousand Irishmen, is guilty of so immense an infidelity so immense a crime against the Irish nation that one can only say of him that it were better for that man (as it were certainly better for his country) that he had not been born.

Ibid.

The student of Irish affairs who does not know Irish literature is ignorant of the awful intensity of the Irish desire for Separation as he is ignorant of one of the chief forces which makes Separation inevitable.

Ibid.

The first man who spoke or seemed to speak for Ireland and who was not Separatist was Henry Grattan. And it was against Henry Grattan's Constitution that Wolfe Tone and the United Irishmen rose. Thus the Pale made common cause with the Gael and declared itself Separatist. It will be conceded that Wolfe Tone was a Separatist; he is *The* Separatist. It will be conceded that Robert Emmet was a Separatist. O'Connell was not a Separatist: but as the United Irishmen revolted against Grattan, Young Ireland revolted against O'Connell. And Young Ireland in its final development was Separatist. To Young Ireland belong three of the great Separatist voices. After Young Ireland the Fenians; and it will be admitted that the Fenians were Separatists. They guarded themselves against future misrepresentation by calling themselves the Irish Republican Brotherhood.

Ibid.

Of Parnell it may be said with absolute truth that he never surrendered the national position.

Ibid.

I have named Tone and Davis and Lalor and Mitchel as the four among us moderns who have chiefly developed the conception of an Irish nation. Others, I have said, have for the most part only interpreted and illustrated what has been taught by these; these are the Fathers and the rest are just their commentarists.

'The Separatist Idea', 1 February, 1916.

Those who have preached the divine wrath of faith and justice and charity and freedom have done so in glorious and imperishable words: and the reason is that God speaks through them. That God spoke to Ireland through Tone and through those who after Tone have taken up his testimony, that Tone's teaching and theirs is true and great and that no other teaching as to Ireland has any truth or worthiness at all is a thing upon which I stake all my mortal and all my immortal hopes. And I ask the men and women of my generation to stake their mortal and immortal hopes with me.

Ibid.

Irish nationality is an ancient spiritual tradition and the Irish nation could not die as long as that tradition lived in the heart of one faithful man or woman. But had the last repositor of the Gaelic tradition, the last unconquered Gael, died, the Irish nation was no more. Any free state that might thereafter be erected in Ireland whatever it might call itself would certainly not be the historic Irish nation.

'The Spiritual Nation', 13 February, 1916.

That Davis would have achieved Irish nationhood by peaceful means if he could is undoubted. Let it not be a reproach against Davis. Obviously if a nation can obtain its freedom without bloodshed it is its duty so to obtain it.

Ibid.

No private right of property is good as against the public right of the nation. But the nation is under a moral obligation so to exercise its public right as to secure strictly equal rights and liberties to every man and woman within the nation.

'The Sovereign People', 31 March, 1916.

Once more, no individual right is good as against the right of the whole people; but the people in exercising its sovereign rights is morally bound to consider individual rights, to do equity between itself and each of the individuals that compose it as well as to see that equity is done between individual and individual.

Ibid

It is for the nation to determine to what extent private property may be held by its members and in what terms of the nation's material resources private property shall be allowed.

Ibid.

Let no man be mistaken as to who will be lord in Ireland when Ireland is free. The people will be lord and master. Mitchel's is the last of the four gospels of the new testament of Irish nationality, the last and the fiercest and the most sublime. It flames with apocalyptic wrath, such wrath as there is nowhere else in literature. And it is because the man loved so well that his wrath is so terrible.

Ibia.

... Mitchel, the least apologetic of men, was at pains to explain that his hate was not of Enlglish men and women but of the English thing which called itself a government in Ireland, of the English Empire, of English commercialism supported by English militarism, a thing wholly evil, perhaps the most evil thing that there has ever been in the world. To talk of such hate as unholy, unchristian, barren is to talk folly or hypocrisy. Such hate is not only a good thing but is a duty.

Ibid.

I admit that I was Commandant-General Commanding-in-Chief of the forces of the Irish Republic which have been acting against you for the past week and that I was President of the Provisional Government. I stand over all my acts and words done or spoken in these capacities. When I was a child of ten I went down on my bare knees by my bedside one night and promised God that I should devote my life to an effort to free my country. I have kept that promise. For among all earthly things as a boy and as a man I have worked for Irish freedom. I have helped to organise, to arm, to train and to discipline my fellow countrymen to the sole end that when the time came they might fight for Irish freedom. The time, as it seemed to me, did come and we went into the fight. I am glad we did. We seem to have lost. We have not lost. To refuse to fight would have been to lose; to fight is to win. We have kept faith with the past and handed a tradition to the future.

*Speech to a secretly held British court martial
in Dublin. 1 or 2 May, 1916.*

I assume that I am speaking to Englishmen who value their own freedom and who profess to be fighting for the freedom of Belgium and Serbia. Believe that we too love freedom and desire it. To us it is more desirable than anything in the world. If you strike us down now we shall rise again and renew the fight. You cannot conquer Ireland; you cannot extinguish the Irish passion for freedom; if our deed has not been sufficient to win freedom then our children will win it by a better deed.

Ibid.

A MOTHER SPEAKS

Dear Mary, that didst see thy first-born Son
Go forth to die amid the scorn of men
For whom He died,
Receive my first-born into thy arms,
Who also hath gone out to die for men,
And keep him by thee till I come to him.
Dear Mary, I have shared thy sorrow,
And soon shall share thy joy.

*Written shortly before his execution
as were the following poems.*

TO MY BROTHER

O faithful!
Moulded in one womb,
We two have stood together all the years,
All the glad years and all the sorrowful years,
Own brothers: through good repute and ill,
In direct peril true to me,
Leaving all things for me, spending yourself
In the hard service that I taught to you,
Of all the men that I have known on earth,
You only have been my familiar friend,
Nor needed I another.

TO MY MOTHER

My gift to you hath been the gift of sorrow,
My one return for your rich gifts to me,
Your gift of life, your gift of love and pity,
Your gift of sanity, your gift of faith
(For who hath had such faith as yours
Since the old time, and what were my poor faith
Without your strong belief to found upon?)
For all these precious things my gift to you
Is sorrow. I have seen
Your dear face line, your face soft to my touch,
Familiar to my hands and to my lips
Since I was little:
I have seen
How you have battled with your tears for me,
And with a proud glad look, although your heart
Was breaking. O Mother (for you know me)

You must have known, when I was silent,
That some strange thing within me kept me dumb,
Some strange deep thing, when I should shout my love?
I have sobbed in secret
For that reserve which yet I could not master,
I would have brought royal gifts, and I have brought you
Sorrow and tears: and yet, it may be
That I have brought you something else besides—
The memory of my deed and of my name
A splendid thing which shall not pass away.
When men speak to me, in praise or in dispraise,
You will not heed, but treasure your own memory
Of your first son.